A Book of Oceanian Writers

The Writers of Australasia, Melanesia, Micronesia & Polynesia

**Please let's know, learn and read the Names of the Best Authors
in
Oceania**

A-Z By Country

Dr. Badal W. Kariye

I

PUBLICATIONS

1. Somali-Português ISBN: 9781304510006 on April 9, 1995, Nairobi, Kenya.by Badal W. Kariye.

2. Af-carabi Af-soomaali "Arabic-Soomaali" ISBN: 978-1-304-03066-5 published on 5th of May, 1996 in Nairobi Kenya by Badal W. Kariye.

3. English-Soomaali “A Teach yourself bilingual Course book,” ISBN: 978-1-304-33282-0 published on on 5th of September, in 1997 by Badal W. Kariye.

4. Baro Tignoolajiga Casriga, May 4, 1997 in Nairobi-Kenya Qore/Writer Badal Kariye

5. Deutsh Soomaali ISBN: ISBN: 978-1-304-33928-7 published on June 25, 1999 in Nairobi, Kenya

6. Helping African Refugees with Small Scale Urban Programs for Survival on January 17, 1998 in Nairobi-Kenya by Badal W. Kariye

7. Ilayska Afafka Af-Soomaali-Français ISBN: 978-1-304-51538-4 "A Teach yourself Bilingual Course book," First Edition published on June

5, 1998 in Nairobi-Kenya by Badal W. Kariye, and Second Edition published on October 6, 2013 in Minneapolis, USA.

8. Français Af-Soomaali ISBN: 978-1-300-97884-8 Un livre de cours bilingues», publié le 5 June 1998, Nairobi, Kenya by Badal W. Kariye (Hunbul)

9. BARO AF-SOOMAALI-ENGLISH ISBN: 978-1-300-97795-7 Published on 20th of February, 1999, Nairobi, Kenya by Badal W. Kariye (Hunbul)

10. Norska-Soomaali Bilingual Course Book ISBN: 978-1-300-98939-4 published on June 25, in 1999, Nairobi Kenya by Badal W. Kariye.

11. KISWAHILI-SOOMAALI Hii kozi Kiswahili kwa lugha mbili-Somali ISBN: 978-1-300-97814-5 kuchapishwa kwenye Juni 25, 1999 Mjini Nairobi, Kenya by Badal W. Kariye (Hunbul) 12. SVENSKA-SOOMAALI ISBN: 9781300978572 Lär Svensk-Somaliska Tvåspråkig kursbok Publicerades Den 15 Mars, 2000 Nairobi, Kenya by Badal W. Kariye (Hunbul)

13. Español-Soomaali ISBN: 978-1-300-98174-9 published on September 15, in 2001, Nairobi Kenya by Badal W. Kariye.

14. OROMIFFA-AF-SOOMAALI ISBN: 978-1-300-97800-8 published on May15, in 2002, Nairobi Kenya by Badal W. Kariye.

15. Português-Somali ISBN: 9781304504272 published on September 9, 2002 in Nairobi, Kenya

16. Italiano-Soomaali ISBN: 978-1-304-34947-7 published on June 12, in 2003, Nairobi Kenya by Badal W. Kariye.

II

17. Swahili-Somali Kamusi ISBN: 978-1-4276-4479-4 "First Bilingual and Plurilingual Dictionary." published on 23th of December, 2009 by Aardvark Global Publishing Inc. Registered in UNESCO ID NO. 186772 - Swahili/Soomaali Kamusi. Af-Sawaaxili/Af-Soomaali Qamuus. Kariye, Badal Salt Lake City, UT, Aardvark Global Publishing, 2009. 545 p. (Plurilingual; Somali, Swahili). Main descriptors: Swahili, Somali, dictionaries Secondary descriptors: African languages CALL NO: D 496.354.493.5 SWA. http://unesdoc.unesco.org/Ulis/cgi-bin/ulis.pl?catno=186772&set=4B69FBEE_3_124&gp=1&lin=1&ll=1 ISBN: 978-1-4276-4479-4

18. The Chopped Love in My Heart ISBN: 978-14276-4448-0 published in 2009 P201 by Salt Lake City, UT, Aardvark Global Publishing, USA.

19. The Genius Lover "We need Family," ISBN: 978-1-4490-8209-3 (sc) ISBN: 978-1-4490-8210-9 (e) published on February 24, 2010 by Author House, USA.

20. The Kaleidoscopic Lover "The Civil War in the Horn of Africa and My Itinerary for a Peace Lover" SBN: 9781452004631 (sc) on July 20, 2010 published by Author House, USA

21. The Political Sociology of Security, Politics, Economics & Diplomacy “Quicker Academic Path for Good Governance ISBN: 9781452085463 (sc) ISBN: 9781452085470 (e) on December 16, 2010 published by Author House, USA.

22. The Queen of Lovers "We need you," ISBN: 9781463415570 published on 1st of January, 2011 by Author House, USA.

23. The Nice Lover "My Interests for Better Future," ISBN: 9781468554199 (sc) published on 17th of February, 2012 by Author House, USA.22. The Lost Lover: I Fed up With the Urbanized Lifestyle Then I Returned to the Countryside for A Wise Bride ISBN-10: 9781477278796/ISBN-13: 978-1477278796 published on 31st October, 2012 by Author House, USA

24. The Nobel Prize “I am the Knowledge Contributor for Literature & Peace in the 21stCentury.”

25. My Official Race To The Office of the Next Secretary-General of the United Nations ISBN: 978-1-304-35835-6 published on August 24, 2013 by Lulu

26. Soomaali-Itaaliano ISBN: 978-1-304-52321-1 published on August 29, 2013 in USA

27. Soomaali-Español ISBN: 978-1-304-51765-4 published on October 7, 2013 in USA

28. Somali-Deutsch ISBN: 9781304520319 published on October 7, 2013 in USA.

29. Soomaali Svenska ISBN: 9781304527189 published on October 9, 2013 in USA

30. SVENSKA ENGLISH “Pocket” ISBN: 978-1-304-54701-9 published on October 17, 2013 in USA.

31. DEUTSCH ENGLISH SOOMAALI ISBN: 978-1-304-54987-7 “Pocket” published on October 19, 2013 in USA.

33. My Official Race To The Post of the Next Secretary-General of the United Nations ISBN: 9781312123236 published on April 21, 2014 in USA

34. A Book of African Writers "Know and Read the Names of the Best African Authors, ISBN: published on June 10, 2014 in USA

35. A Book of South & North American Writers ISBN: 978-1-312-26849-4 published on June 10, 2014 in USA

36. A Book of European Writers, ISBN: 978-1-312-27415-0 published on June 12, 2014 in USA

37. A Book of Oceanian Writers ISBN: 978-1-312-27773-1 published on June 14, 2014 in USA

38. I am currently writing a new book about "The Cyber War We're within".

A Note from the Author

I am Ambassador Dr. Badal W. Kariye "Dr. Hunbul" the author and the copyright owner of this beloved, enjoyable and guideline book for the names of Oceanian authors.

I was born in the Democratic Republic of Somalia where I fled from the civil war in 1991 to neighboring Kenya where I've been living as a refugee then I immigrated to the United States of America on 26the of September, 2006 where I became American Citizen. I really love my new and second homeland - The United States of America (USA).

I traveled more countries than any other authors/writers as a refugee, researcher, journalist, security expert and multilateral diplomat who wanted to solve any tribal and political conflicts while I have had the interests to master languages and contribute knowledge in literature and peace to humanity. I love to meet people and share knowledge for better solutions.

I wish my fellow world writers to simplify how to read literature rather than hardening it because many of our global citizens do not know or understand how to win to write or read, and we must teach everyone how to read write and read.

As the internationally renowned Somali/African American scholar and writer who wrote some of the best books in this planetary globe. My visionary mission isn't to get rich or to be a famous person but I just want to leave valuable books which many generations can and will benefit to read, study, understand it clearly and wisely therefore; they can serve and contribute knowledge honestly to humanity.

I'll always contribute knowledge to humanity if and when I can, and I like to offer my enriched wisdom and knowledge contributions in order to share with our global citizens, writers, and scholars around the globe.

God bless Africa! God bless the United States of America! God bless the World!

Preface

This guideline book is based on the facts of the let's know, learn and read the Names of the Best Oceanian Authors & their wonderful contributions in literary work and literature.

The Oceanian people are very rich for everything but most of the Oceanian people may not stop to concentrate even if they are contributing knowledge to humanity, and we must use common sense and encourage to those who can excel and show extraordinary achievements of any kind.

Let's learn, write, read or listen to whatever we can achieve.

Welcome to know the Writers of Oceania

Contents

1

Chapter 1

Australian Writers

A

Azhar Abidi (born 1968) Passarola Rising (2006), Twilight (2008), The House of Bilqis (2009)
Glenda Adams (1939–2007) Games of the Strong (1982), Longleg (1990), The Tempest of Clemenza (1996), Miles Franklin Award winner (1987) for Dancing on Coral
Debra Adelaide (born 1958) The Hotel Albatross (1995), Serpent Dust (1998), The Household Guide to Dying (2008)
Alexandra Adornetto (born 1992) The Strangest Adventures series
Malcolm Afford (1906–1954) The Gland Men of the Island (Wonder Stories pp. 828–843, January 1931), Blood on His Hands!: A Detective Novel (1936), Death's Mannikins: Being a Sober Account of Certain Diabolical Happenings not Untinged with the Odour of Brimstone which Befell a Respectable Family Living at Exmoor in This Present Year (1937), The Dead Are Blind: A Jeffrey Blackburn Adventure (1937), Fly By Night: A Jeffrey Blackburn Adventure (1942), Owl of Darkness (1944), Sinners in Paradise (1946), The Sheep and the Wolves (1947), The Vanishing Trick, Detective Fiction 1.1 (1948), Such a Neat Little Corpse (1950?)
Maggie Alderson (born 1959) Pants on Fire (2000), Mad About the Boy (2002), Handbags and Gladrags (2004), Cents and Sensibility (2006), How to Break Your Own Heart (2008), Shall We Dance (2010), Evangeline: The Wish Keeper's Helper (2011), Everything Changes But You (2012)
James Aldridge (born 1918) Signed with Their Honour (1942), The Sea Eagle (1944), The Diplomat (1949), The Hunter (1950), Heroes of the Empty View (1954), I Wish He Would Not Die (1957), A Captive in the Land (1962), My Brother Tom (1966), The Untouchable Juli (1974), Mockery In Arms (1974), The Marvellous Mongolian (1974), One Last Glimpse (1977), Goodbye Un-America (1979), The Broken SaddleThe True Story of Lilli Stubeck (1984), The True Story of Spit Macphee (1986) (winner of the Guardian Prize and New South Wales Premier's Literary Award), The True Story of Lola Mackellar (Viking, 1992), The Girl from the Sea (2002), The Wings of Kitty St Clair (2006)
Ethel Anderson (1883–1958) Indian Tales (1948), At Parramatta (1956), The Little Ghosts (1959)
Jessica Anderson (1916–2010) An Ordinary Lunacy (1963), The Last Man's Head (1970), The Commandant (1975), The Impersonators (1980), Miles Franklin Literary Award winner in 1978 for Tirra Lirra by the River and in 1980 for The Impersonators), Taking Shelter (1989), One of the Wattle Birds (1994)
Sarah Armstrong (born 1968) Miles Franklin Literary Award nominee 2005 (Salt Rain)
Wayne Ashton (born 1959) Under a Tin-Grey Sari (2002), Equator: A Novel (2010)
Thea Astley (1925–2004) Girl with a Monkey (1958), A Descant for Gossips (1960), The Well Dressed Explorer (1962), The Slow Natives (1965), A Boat Load of Home Folk (1968), The Acolyte (1972), A Kindness Cup (1974), An Item from the Late News (1982), Beachmasters (1985), It's Raining in Mango (1987), Reaching Tin River (1990), Vanishing Points (1992), Coda (1994), The Multiple Effects of Rainshadow (1996), Drylands (1999), Miles Franklin Literary Award winner in 1999 for Drylands, 1972 for The Acolyte, 1965 for The Slow Natives, and 1962 for The Well Dressed Explorer
Hugh Atkinson (1924–1994) The Pink and the Brown (1957), Low Company(1961), The Reckoning (1963), The Games (1968), The Most Savage Animal (1972), Johnny Horns (1972), The Man in the Middle (1973), Crack-up (1974), Weekend to Kill (1977), Unscheduled Flight (1978),

The Manipulators (1978), Billy Two-Toes (1982), Grey's Valley: The Legend (1986), A Twist in the Tale: Three Novellas (1991), Jumping Jeweller of Lavender Bay (1992)
Louisa Atkinson (1834–1872) Gertrude the Emigrant: A Tale of Colonial Life by an Australian Lady (1857), Cowanda: The Veteran's Grant: an Australian Story by the Author of Gertrude (1859), Debatable Ground of the Carlillawarra Claimants (1861), Myra (1864), Tom Hellicar's Children (1871), Bush Home (?), Tressa's Resolve (1872)
Bunty Avieson (born 1962) Apartment 255 (2002), The Wrong Door(2004)
B
Murray Bail (born 1941) Homesickness (1980), Holden's Performance (1987), Miles Franklin Literary Award winner 1999 for Eucalyptus (1998), The Pages (2008), The Voyage (2012)
Allan Baillie (born 1943) Creature (1987), Mates and Other Stories (1989), Dream Catcher and Other Stories (1995), The Phone Book (1995), Ten Out of Ten (2003), A Taste of Cockroach (2005)
Faith Bandler (born 1918) Wacvie (1977)
Marjorie Barnard (1897–1987) The Persimmon Tree, and Other Stories (1943), (As M. Barnard Eldershaw) A House is Built (1929)', Green Memory (1931), The Glasshouse (1936), Plaque with Laurel (1937), Tomorrow and Tomorrow and Tomorrow (1945)
John Arthur Barry (1850–1911) The Luck of the Native Born (1898), A Son of the Sea (1899)
Max Barry (born 1973) Syrup (1999), Jennifer Government (2003), Company (2006)
Catherine Bateson (born 1960) A Dangerous Girl (2000), The Year It All Happened (2001), Painted Love Letters (2002), His Name is Fire (2006)
Barbara Baynton (1862–1929) Human Toll (1907)
George Lewis Becke (1855–1913)
Randolph Bedford (1868–1941) True Eyes and the Whirlwind (1903), The Snare of Strength (1905), Sops of Wine (1909), Billy Pagan Mining Engineer (1911), The Mates of Torres (1911), The Lady of the Pickup (1911), The Silver Star (1917), Aladdin and the Boss Cockie (1919)
Larissa Behrendt (born 1969) Home (2004), Legacy (2009)
Barbara Biggs (born 1956) Chat Room (2006)
Carmel Bird (born 1940) Cherry Ripe (1986), Bluebird Cafe (1990), The White Garden (1996), Crisis (1996), Red Shoes (1998), Unholy Writ (2000), Open for Inspection (2002), Cape Grimm (2005), Child of the Twilight (2010)
John Birmingham (born 1964) Axis of Time trilogy (publication commenced 2004), He Died with a Felafel in His Hand (1994)
Marie Bjelke-Petersen (1874–1969) The Captive Singer (1917), The Immortal Flame (1919), Dusk: A Novel (1921), Jewelled Nights (1923), The Moon Minstrel (1927), Monsoon Music (1930), The Rainbow Lute (1932), The Silver Knight (1934), Jungle Night (1937)
Georgia Blain (born 1964)
Capel Boake (1889–1944) Painted Clay (1917), The Romany Mark (1923), The Dark Thread (1936), As the Twig is Bent (1946)
Merlinda Bobis (born 1959) Filipino expatriate. Banana Heart Summer (2005); also poet
Rolf Boldrewood (Thomas Alexander Browne) (1826–1915) My Run Home (1874), The Squatter's Dream: A Story of Australian Life (1875), A Colonial Reformer (1876), Babes in the Bush (1877), Robbery Under Arms (1882), The Sealskin Coat (1884–1885), The Crooked Stick, or, Pollie's Probation (1885), The Sphinx of Eaglehawk: A Tale of Old Bendigo (1887), A Sydney-Side Saxon (1888), Nevermore (1889–90), The Miner's Right: A Tale of the Australian Goldfields (1890),

A Modern Buccaneer (1894), Plain Living: A Bush Idyll (1898), War to the Knife', or Tangata Maori (1899), The Ghost-Camp, or, The Avengers (1902)', The Last Chance: A Tale of the Golden West (1905)
Guy Boothby (1867–1905) Doctor Nikola series
Martin Boyd (1893–1972) Brangane: A Memoir (by Martin Mills, pseudonym) (1926); The Picnic (1937), Lucinda Brayford (1946), The "Langton" quartet: The Cardboard Crown (1952); A Difficult Young Man (1955); Outbreak of Love (1957); When Blackbirds Sing (1962)
Russell Braddon (1921–1995) The Naked Island
James Bradley (born 1967) Wrack (1997); The Deep Field (1999), The Resurrectionist (2006)
Lily Brett (born 1946) Things Could Be Worse (1990), What God Wants (1992), Just Like That (1994), Too Many Men (2001), You Gotta Have Balls (2006), Lola Bensky (2013)
Paul Brickhill (1916–1991) WWII RAAF fighter pilot, The Great Escape] (1950)
Damien Broderick (born 1944) Science fiction The Judas Mandala
Steve Brook (born 1934) Polish-born journalist and satirical novelist
Geraldine Brooks (born 1955) Pulitzer Prize for fiction, 2006: March (2005); Year of Wonders (2001), also Pulitzer Prize winning journalist
Carter Brown (1923–1985) Crime fiction
Anna Maria Bunn (1808–1889) The Guardian. A Tale (1838)
Janine Burke (born 1952) Speaking (1984), Second Sight (1986), Company of Images (1989), Lullaby (1994)
C
Kathleen Caffyn (c. 1855 – 1926)
Mena Calthorpe (c. 1905 – 1996)
Ada Cambridge (1844–1926)
Marion May Campbell (born 1948)
Rosa Campbell Praed (1851–1935)
Trudi Canavan (born 1969)
Rosa Cappiello (born 1942)
Gabrielle Carey (born 1959) Puberty Blues
Peter Carey (born 1943) Illywhacker, Oscar and Lucinda, twice Booker Prize Winner and three time Miles Franklin Award winner
Isobelle Carmody (born 1958) The Gathering (1993)
Steven Carroll (born 1949)
Jay Caselberg Science fiction
Gavin Casey (1907–1964)
Belinda Castles (born 1971) The River Baptists 2006 Australian/Vogel Literary Award winner
Brian Castro (born 1950)
Nancy Cato (1917–2000)
Nick Cave (born 1957)
Arlene J. Chai (born 1955)
Joy Chambers
Nan Chauncy (1900–1970)
Margaret Clark (born 1942) Fat Chance (1996)
Marcus Clarke (1846–1881) For the Term of his Natural Life
James Clavell (1924–1994) Shogun also screenwriter, director (the original The Fly).

Jon Cleary (born 1917)
Inga Clendinnen (born 1934) Reading the Holocaust (1999); Dancing with Strangers (2004);
Charmian Clift (1923–1969)
Jane Clifton (born 1961)
J. M. Coetzee (born 1940) South African born writer who emigrated to Australia in 2002, and became an Australian citizen in 2006
Bernard Cohen (born 1963) The Blindman's Hat 1996 Australian/Vogel Literary Award winner
Tom Collins Such Is Life see Joseph Furphy below.
Kenneth Cook (1929–1987) Wake in Fright
Jill Ker Conway (born 1934)
Peter Corris (born 1942) Crime fiction
Bryce Courtenay (born 1933) The Power of One
Jessie Catherine Couvreur (1848–1897)
Bernard Cronin (1884–1968)
Zora Cross (1890–1964)
Dymphna Cusack (1902–1981)
D
John Bede Dalley (1878–1935)
Eleanor Dark (1901–1985) Prelude to Christopher, The Timeless Land
Helen Darville (Helen Demidenko) (born 1972) The Hand That Signed the Paper 1993
Luke Davies (born 1962)
Frank Dalby Davison (1893–1970)
Eric Dando (born 1970) satirical novels Snail and Oink, Oink, Oink
Liam Davison (born 1957)
Carlton Dawe (1865–1935)
Dulcie Deamer (1890–1972)
Joel Deane (born 1969)
Kathryn Deans children's fantasy
Ralph De Boissière (born 1907)
Michelle de Kretser The Hamilton Case
Meaghan Delahunt (born 1961)
Kit Denton (1928–1997) The Breaker
Robert Dessaix (born 1944) Night Letters (1996)
James Devaney (1890–1976)
Jean Devanny (1894–1962)
András Domahidy (born 1920) Writes in Hungarian
Henrietta Drake-Brockman (1901–1968) Men Without Wives
Sara Dowse
Robert Drewe (born 1943) Our Sunshine (1991)
Ursula Dubosarsky (born 1961)
Alasdair Duncan (born 1982)
Mary Durack (1913–1994) Kings in Grass Castles
E
Nick Earls (born 1963)
Arabella Edge The Company: The Story of a Murderer

Greg Egan (born 1961) Science fiction
Flora Eldershaw (1897–1956)
M. Barnard Eldershaw pseudonym for Flora Eldershaw and Marjorie Barnard
Sumner Locke Elliott (1917–1991) Careful, He Might Hear You
Matilda Jane Evans (1827–1886)
F
Michel Faber (born 1960) The Crimson Petal and the White
Delia Falconer (born 1966)
Jennifer Fallon (born 1959) Fantasy
Margaret Fane (1887-1962) novelist and poet
Beverley Farmer (born 1941) The House in the Light
Helen FitzGerald (born 1966) novelist and screenwriter, Dead Lovely (2007)
John Flanagan (born 1944) Ranger's Apprentice
Penny Flanagan (born 1970)
Richard Flanagan (born 1961) Gould's Book of Fish
Tom Flood (born 1955) Oceana Fine
David Foster (born 1944) The Glade Within the Grove (1997) Miles Franklin Award
Mabel Forrest (1872–1935)
Miles Franklin (1879–1954) My Brilliant Career Her estate led to creation of the Miles Franklin Award
Jackie French (born 1953)
Mary Eliza Fullerton (1868–1946)
Joseph Furphy (1843–1912) Such Is Life. Nom de plume 'Tom Collins'
G
Antonella Gambotto-Burke (born 1965)
Helen Garner (born 1942), Monkey Grip, The Children's Bach, The Spare Room
Mary Gaunt (1861–1942)
Nikki Gemmell (born 1966), The Bride Stripped Bare
Ruby Langford Ginibi (born 1934)
Alan Gold (born 1945), historical novels
Andrea Goldsmith (born 1950)
Peter Goldsworthy (born 1951) Honk If You are Jesus (1992)
Alan Gould (born 1949), To the Burning City, also poet
Nathaniel Gould (1857–1919)
Posie Graeme-Evans (born 1952)
Richard Harry Graves (1898–1971)
Evan Green (1930–1996)
Kerry Greenwood (born 1954), crime fiction
Kate Grenville (born 1950) The Idea of Perfection (2001) Orange Prize for FictionThe Secret River (2006) Commonwealth Writers' Prize
Dick Gross (born 1954)
Mrs Aeneas Gunn (Jeannie Gunn) (1870–1961), We of the Never Never
H
Alfred Arthur Greenwood Hales (1860–1936)
Rodney Hall (born 1935) Just Relations (1982), The Grisly Wife (1994) Miles Franklin Award; The Day We Had Hitler Home
Marion Halligan (born 1940)

Rosalie Ham (born 1955)
Lyn Hancock; (born 1938)
Derek Hansen (born 1944)
Lee Harding (born 1937) Science fiction
Traci Harding Fantasy.
Frank Hardy (1917–1994) Power Without Glory
Alexander Harris (1805–1874)
Elizabeth Harrower (born 1928) The Long Prospect
Sonya Hartnett (born 1968)
John Harwood (born 1946)
Nicholas Hasluck (born 1944)
Shirley Hazzard (born 1931) The Transit of Venus (1980) National Book Critics Circle Award, The Great Fire (2003) Miles Franklin Award.
Ruth Hegarty (born 1929) Is That You Ruthie?
Rolf Heimann (born 1940)
Anita Heiss (born 1968)
John David Hennessey (1847–1935)
Mark Henshaw (born 1951)
Xavier Herbert (1901–1984) Poor Fellow My Country
Dorothy Hewett (1923–2002) Also poet & playwright
Kathryn Heyman (born 1965)
Jennifer Higgie
Helen Hodgman (born 1945) Broken Words (1989) Christina Stead Fiction Prize
Chloe Hooper (born 1973)
Janette Turner Hospital (born 1942) Oyster (1996)
Fergus Hume (1859–1932)
Maria Hyland (born 1968) Carry Me Down
I
David Ireland (born 1927) A Woman of the Future (1979), The Glass Canoe (1976) Miles Franklin Award
Ian Irvine (born 1950)
J
Antoni Jach (1956) Napoleon's Double, The Weekly Card Game, The Layers of the City.
Annamarie Jagose (born 1965) Slow Water.
Florence James (1902–1993) co-author Come In Spinner with Dymphna Cusack
Winifred Lewellin James (1876–1941)
Charlotte Jay (Geraldine Halls) (1919–1996) Crime fiction, Beat Not the Bones.
Barbara Jefferis (1917–2004)
Kate Jennings (born 1948) Moral Hazard.
Paul Jennings. (born 1943) Children's literature Wicked! (1998)
Dorothy Johnston (born 1948)
George Johnston (1912–1970) My Brother Jack.
Martin Johnston (1947–1990) Mainly poet.
Elizabeth Jolley (1923–2007) The Well (1986) Miles Franklin Award
Gail Jones (born 1955)

Rae Desmond Jones (born 1941)
Rod Jones (born 1953)
Nicholas Jose (born 1952) Paper Nautilus, The Rose Crossing,The Custodians, The Red Thread.
K
Christopher Kelen (born 1958) Also poet & artist
Thomas Keneally (born 1935) Schindler's Ark (1985) Booker Prize winner, filmed as Schindler's List; Bring Larks and Heroes (1967) and Three Cheers for the Paraclete (1968) Miles Franklin Award winners
Cate Kennedy (born 1963) The World Beneath
Robin Klein (born 1936)
Christopher Koch (born 1932) The Doubleman (1985) and Highways to a War (1996) Miles Franklin Award winners
Torsten Krol
L
Eric Lambert (1918–1966)
John Lang (1817–1864)
Eve Langley (1908–1974)
Coral Lansbury (1929–1991)
Henry George Lamond (1885–1969)
Justine Larbalestier young adult fantasy, Magic or Madness (2005)
William Lawson (1876–1957)
Simone Lazaroo
Kathy Lette (born 1958) Puberty Blues (1979) Girls' Night Out (1988)
Joan Lindsay (1896–1984)
Norman Lindsay (1879–1969) The Magic Pudding. Also a noted artist.
Hilary Lofting (1881-1939) short story and travel writing
Amanda Lohrey (born 1947)
Joan London (born 1958)
Gabrielle Lord (born 1946) Crime fiction
Angelo Loukakis The Memory of Tides (2006)
Melissa Lucashenko
Dave Luckett (born 1951) children's fantasy, A Dark Winter (1997)
Morris Lurie (born 1938) Seven Books for Grossman (1983), Patrick White Award 2006
M
Catherine Edith Macauley Martin (born 1847–1937)
N.R Marxsen (born 1988)
Mardi McConnochie (born 1971)
Colleen McCullough (born 1937) The Thorn Birds
Sandy McCutcheon (born 1947)
Meme McDonald
Roger McDonald (born 1941) Miles Franklin Award winner for The Ballad of Desmond Kale
Andrew McGahan (born 1966) Miles Franklin Award winner for The White Earth
Fiona McGregor (born 1965) Age Book of the Year winner for Indelible Ink
Emily Maguire (born 1976)
Hugh Mackay

Kenneth Seaforth Mackenzie (1913–1955) Dead Men Rising
Ronald McKie (1909–1991) Miles Franklin Award winner for The Mango Tree
Jennifer Maiden (born 1949)
Shane Maloney Crime fiction
David Malouf (born 1934) Miles Franklin Award winner for The Great World
Leonard Mann (1895–1981)
Frederic Manning (1882–1935)
Kathleen Mannington Caffyn (Circa 1855–1926)
Melina Marchetta (born 1965) Looking For Alibrandi
John Marsden (born 1950) Best known for the Tomorrow series.
William Leonard Marshall (born 1944) Detective fiction. Yellowthread Street
Olga Masters (1919–1986)
Peter Mathers (1931–2004) Miles Franklin Award winner for Trap
Gillian Mears (born 1964) The Grass Sister Commonwealth Writers Prize (Regional) 1996
Louisa Anne Meredith (1812–1895)
Alex Miller (born 1936) Miles Franklin Award winner for The Ancestor Game and Journey to the Stone Country
Drusilla Modjeska (born 1946) The Orchard (1994)
Ian Moffitt (1926–2000)
James Moloney (born 1954)
Frank Moorhouse (born 1938) Miles Franklin Award winner for Dark Palace
Sally Morgan (born 1951) My Place
Jaclyn Moriarty Young adult fiction.
Mudrooroo (formerly Colin Johnson) (born) Wild Cat Falling
Gerald Murnane (born 1939)
Joanna Murray-Smith (born 1962) Judgement Rock
N
Alice Nannup (1911–1995) When the Pelican Laughed
Simpson Newland (1835–1925)
Nerida Newton (born 1972) The Lambing Flat
John Henry Nicholson (1838–1923)
D'Arcy Niland (1919–1967) The Shiralee
Hume Nisbet (1849–1923)
Michael Noonan (1921–2000) The December Boys
Louis Nowra (born 1950) Better known as a playwright
Judy Nunn (born 1945)
O
Andrew T. O'Connor (born 1978) Tuvalu
Elizabeth O'Conner (born 1913) The Irishman, 1960 Miles Franklin Award winner
John O'Grady (1907–1981) They're a Weird Mob
Wendy Orr Canadian-born Australian children's writer, of Nim's Island and others
Ouyang Yu (born 1955) Expatriate Chinese, also poet and editor.
P
Margaret Packham Hargrave (born 1941) A Woman of Air
Vance and Nettie Palmer Also dramatists and critics.

Ruth Park (born 1923) The Harp in the South
Pyotr Patrushev (born 1942) Project Nirvana
Elliot Perlman (born 1964) Three Dollars
James Phelan (born 1979) "Literati", "Fox Hunt", "Patriot Act", "Blood Oil".
Nancy Phelan (born 1913) Also memoirist, 2004 Patrick White Award winner
D.B.C. Pierre (born 1961) 2003 Booker Prize winner for Vernon God Little
Doris Pilkington Garimara (born 1937) Follow the Rabbit-Proof Fence
Dorothy Porter (1954–2008) Verse novels, The Monkey's Mask
Hal Porter (1911–1984) The Tilted Cross, Better known for memoir The Watcher on the Cast Iron Balcony
Rosa Campbell Praed (1851–1935)
Katharine Susannah Prichard (1883–1969) The Goldfields Trilogy, The Roaring Nineties (1946) etc.
Boori Monty Prior
R
Matthew Reilly (born 1974) Action/thriller
Henry Handel Richardson (aka. Ethel Robertson) (1870–1946) The Fortunes of Richard Mahony
Gregory David Roberts (born 1952) Shantaram
Peter Robb (born 1946) Midnight in Sicily M
Deborah Robertson (born 1959) Careless
Alice Grant Rosman (1882–1961)
Jennifer Rowe (Emily Rodda) (born 1948) Crime fiction & children's fantasy, Deltora Quest.
Penelope Rowe (born 1946)
Tracy Ryan (born 1964) Novelist, poet and translator
S
Eva Sallis (born 1964) (Eva Hornung) Haim (1997) Australian/Vogel Literary Award
Philip Salom (born 1950) Also poet
G K Saunders (born 1910) The Stranger
Georgia Savage
Henry Savery (1791–1842) Convicted forger and Australia's first novelist
Conrad Sayce (1888–1935) Outback adventure novels
Wendy Scarfe (born 1933) Novelist, biographer and poet
Katherine Scholes (born 1959) The Stone Angel
John A. Scott (born 1948) Also poet, Warra Warra, What I Have Written (1994)
Kim Scott (born 1957) Benang
Rosie Scott (born 1948)
Alan Seymour (born 1927) Mainly playwright
Thomas Shapcott (born 1935) Poet, novelist and playwright, 2000 Patrick White Award winner
Charles Herbert Shaw (1900–1955) Journalist and detective fiction
Patricia Shaw (born 1929) River of the Sun (1991) and The Opal Seekers (1996)
Nevil Shute (1899–1960) A Town Like Alice (1950), On the Beach (1957)
Craig Silvey (born 1982) Rhubarb (2004), Jasper Jones (2009)
Helen de Guerry Simpson (1897–1940)
Catherine Helen Spence (1825–1910) Clara Morison: A Tale of South Australia During the Gold Fever (1854)

Lindsay Simpson (born 1957) Crime fiction
Tim Sinclair (born 1972)
Eleanor Spence (born 1928–2008) Young adults author
Ken Spillman (born 1959)
Kimberley Starr (born 1970) The Kingdom Where Nobody Dies
Nicolette Stasko (born 1950) The Invention of Everyday Life (2007)
Christina Stead (1902–1983) The Man Who Loved Children (1940), For Love Alone (1945), Letty Fox: Her Luck (1946)
Gordon Neil Stewart (1912–1999) Crime fiction
Madeleine St John (1941–2006) Booker Prize for Fiction shortlisted The Essence of the Thing (1997)
Dal Stivens (1911–1997) Jimmy Brockett 1981 Patrick White Award winner
Louis Stone (1871–1935) Jonah
Randolph Stow (born 1935) To the Islands (1958) Miles Franklin Award; Patrick White Award (1979); The Merry-Go-Round in the Sea (1965)
Donald Stuart (1913–1983) Yandy
T
Peter Temple (born 1946) Crime fiction, The Broken Shore (2005), The Truth (2009), winner of the Miles Franklin Literary Award (2010)
Kylie Tennant (1912–1988) The Battlers (1941), Ride on Stranger (1943)
Colin Thiele (1920–2006) Storm Boy (1964)
Carrie Tiffany (born 1965) Everyman's Rules for Scientific Living (2005), shortlisted for the Miles Franklin Literary Award and the Orange Prize; Mateship with Birds (2012)
P. L. Travers (1899–1996) Mary Poppins (1934)
Rachael Treasure Jillaroo (2000)
Penelope Trevor (born 1960) Listening for Small Sounds (1996)
Christos Tsiolkas (born 1965) Loaded (1995); Dead Europe (2005); The Slap (2008), winner of Best Book Commonwealth Writers Prize 2009, shortlisted for Miles Franklin Literary Award (2009)
Lee Tulloch Fabulous Nobodies
Ethel Turner (1872–1958) Seven Little Australians (1894)
George Turner (1916–1997) The Cupboard Under the Stairs (1962) Miles Franklin Award
U
Arthur Upfield (1890–1964) Crime fiction featuring the part-aboriginal detective 'Boney'; The Sands of Windee (1931)
V
Lin Van Hek
Frederick Bert Vickers (1903–????)
Mary Theresa Vidal (1815–1869)
Paul Voermans (1960) Science fiction
W
Brenda Walker (born 1957) The Wing of Night
Dave Warner (born 1953) Crime fiction
Judah Waten (1912–1985)
E. L. Grant Watson (1885–1970)
Sam Watson (born 1952) The Kadaitcha Sung
Archie Weller (born 1957) The Day of the Dog

Morris West (1916–1999) The Shoes of the Fisherman
Herb Wharton (born 1936)
Nadia Wheatley (born 1949) Children's fiction
Patrick White (1912–1990) Winner of Nobel Prize for Literature (1973) for The Eye of the Storm; inaugural winner, Miles Franklin Award 1957 – Voss.
Sonny Whitelaw (born 1956) Science fiction, (Stargate series)
Lili Wilkinson (born 1981)
Eric Willmot (born 1936)
Darren Williams (born 1967) Angel Rock, 1994 Australian/Vogel Literary Award winner
Anne Wilson (1848–1930)
Ben Winch (born 1973)
Tara June Winch (1983) Swallow the Air
Gerard Windsor (born 1944) Heaven Where The Bachelors Sit
Tim Winton (born 1960) Miles Franklin Award winner 1984 Shallows, 1992 Cloudstreet, 2002 Dirt Music, 2009 Breath
Amy Witting (1918–2001) I for Isobel, 1993 Patrick White Award winner
Charlotte Wood (born 1965) The Submerged Cathedral
Sue Woolfe (born 1950) Leaning Towards Infinity
Alexis Wright (born 1950) Carpentaria 2007 Miles Franklin Award winner
Patricia Wrightson (1921–2010) children's author, The Rocks of Honey (1960), An Older Kind of Magic (1972), The Nargun and the Stars (1973)
Y
Morgan Yasbincek (born 1964)
Z
Markus Zusak (born 1975) The Book Thief

Christmas Island Writers (Australasia)

Unknown Writers

Cocos (Keeling) Islands Writers (Australasia)

Unknown Writers

Coral Sea Islands Writers (Australasia)

Unknown Writers

Norfolk Island Writers (Australasia)

Alice Buffett
Peter Clarke
Archie Bigg

Coleen McCulough
Bob Tofts
Merval Haore
Nau Smith
Maev & Gil Hitch

Chapter 2

New Zealand Writers

Frank Oswald Victor Acheson
Catherine Mary Ann Adamson
George Alderton
William Frederick Alexander
Colin Allan
Harry Howard Barton Allan
Geoffrey Thomas Alley
Frank Sheldon Anthony
Sylvia Ashton-Warner
Kenneth Stopford Avery
Charles John Ayton
Wilhelmina Sherriff Bain
David Paton Balfour
Alfred Richard Barclay
Barry Barclay
Mary Anne Barker
Sarah Maria Barraud
William Jackson Barry
Ottavio Barsanti
John Saxon Barton
Alexander Bathgate
Blanche Edith Baughan
Arthur Baysting
Bernard Beckett
George Bell (editor)
James Abbott Mackintosh Bell
Francis Oswald Bennett
Joe Bennett (writer)
Leo Vernon Bensemann
Victor Billot
David Bishop
Ellen Wright Blackwell
James Bodell
George Wallace Bollinger
Kerry Bolton
Costa Botes
Avice Maud Bowbyes
Riwia Brown
Harriet Louisa Browne
Bryan Bruce

John Cairney (anatomist)
Arnold Everitt Campbell
Una Isabel Carter
John Caselberg
Bruce Cathie
Hannah Rebecca Frances Caverhill
Tim Chadwick
William Chapple
Nellie Euphemia Coad
Frank Livingstone Combs
Jennifer Compton
Sandra Coney
William Douglas Cook
James Copland
Bessie Lee Cowie
Daryl Crimp
Barry Crump
Eveline Willett Cunnington
Dan Davin
Winnie Davin
Charles Oliver Bond Davis
Esmond Samuel de Beer
Joan de Hamel
Thomas Denniston
Arthur Desmond
Bill Direen
Herbert Boucher Dobbie
Alexander Don
Thomas Edward Donne
Alan Duff
George Edgecumbe
Samuel Edger
Martin Edmond
Edwin Edwards (New Zealand politician)
Howard Leslie Elliott
James Sands Elliott
Ellen Elizabeth Ellis
Brian Falkner (author)
Outhwaite Family, Auckland
Roderick David Finlayson
Cedric Firth
Percy Leo Fowler
Margaret Fraser
Philadelphus Bain Fraser
Catherine Fulton

Norah Telford Burnard
Kurt Gänzl
Mario Gaoa
Elizabeth Anne Gard'ner
Frances Shayle George
Charlotte Godley
Paul Goldsmith (politician)
Briar Grace-Smith
Sarah Greenwood (artist)
Herbert Guthrie-Smith
Octavius Hadfield
Mandy Hager
Roger Hall
George Hamilton-Browne
Jane Elizabeth Harris
Craig Harrison (writer)
Florence Marie Harsant
Adrian Hayter
Joseph William Allan Heenan
Andrew Kennaway Henderson
Christina Kirk Henderson
Ellen Anne Hewett
Eva Esther Hill
Alfred George Horton
Edith Annie Howes
Ihaia Hutana
Catherine Lucy Innes
Fanny Louise Irvine-Smith
Florence James
Samuel Johnson (New Zealand editor)
Pei Te Hurinui Jones
Rangi Ruru Wananga Karaitiana
Hamish Keith
James Kelly (priest)
Anne Kennedy
Thomas Kirk (botanist)
Ante Kosovich
Adrian Cornelius Langerwerf
William John Larkin
Leonard Poulter Leary
John A. Lee
Samuel Lister (editor)
Ronald Lockley
Ida Mary Lough
Edith Joan Lyttleton

John MacGregor (New Zealand politician)
Hester Maclean
Leo Madigan
Sam Mahon
Hamuera Tamahau Mahupuku
Purakau Maika
Emilie Monson Malcolm
Frederick Edward Maning
George Edward Mannering
James Henry Marriott
Mary Ann Martin
Bruce Mason
Joseph Masters
Sarah Louise Mathew
Clive Matthew-Wilson
Muriel Wallace May
Ossie Mazengarb
Anthony McCarten
Lancelot William McCaskill
Dennis McEldowney
Shona McFarlane
Greg McGee
Ronald Alexander McIntosh
Peter McIntyre (artist)
Arthur McKee
David McKinney (author)
Alexander McMinn
James Anderson McPherson
William Perrett Mead
Richard Meros
O. E. Middleton
Alexander Miller (theologian)
Harry Louis Moffatt
Geoff Moon
Edward George Britton Moss
Ryan Nelsen
New Zealand Post Katherine Mansfield Prize
Keith Newman (writer)
Carl Nixon
Percy Reginald Paris
Ruth Park
Neville Peat
Alfred Philpott
Tama Poata
Joel Samuel Polack

Brent Pope (rugby analyst)
James Henry Pope
Jeremy Pope
Hemi Potatau
Alexander Wyclif Reed
Alfred Hamish Reed
Annie Lee Rees
Amber Reeves
Magdalene Stuart Reeves
Harold Winston Rhodes
Mary Elizabeth Richmond
Mike Riddell
Ken Ring (writer)
Lauren Kim Roche
Ettie Annie Rout
Tania Roxborogh
Dhanish Semar
Verpal Singh
Barry Smith (preacher)
Glenn Standring
Keith Steele
Bruce Stewart (playwright)
William Downie Stewart, Jr.
Fleur Adcock
Barbara Anderson
K O Arvidson
Murray Ball
Mary Anne Barker (Lady Barker)
James K. Baxter
Bernard Beckett
James Belich
Ivan Bootham
Jenny Bornholdt
Thomas Bracken
Charles Brasch
Errol Brathwaite
Fleur Beale
Alistair Campbell
Meg Campbell
Ken Catran
Eleanor Catton
Deborah Challinor
Gordon Challis
Catherine Chidgey
Paul Cleave

Hugh Cook
Joy Cowley
Barry Crump
Allen Curno
Dan Davin
George E. Dewar
William Direen (Bill Direen)
Lynley Dodd
Alfred Domett
Joan Druett
Marilyn Duckworth
Tessa Duder
Alan Duff
Eileen Duggan[citation needed]
Maurice Duggan
Kate Duignan
Stevan Eldred-Grigg
Chris Else
Barbara Ewing
Fiona Farrell
Janet Frame
Ruth France
Maurice Gee
Ivy Gibbs
Denis Glover
Patricia Grace
H. W. Gretton
Roger Hall
J. H. Haslam
Kathleen Hawkins
Joel Hayward
M. H. Holcroft
Keri Hulme
Sam Hunt
Rex Hunter
Robin Hyde
Witi Ihimaera
Andrew Johnston
Lloyd Jones
Tim Jones
V. M. Jones
Fiona Kidman
Michael King
Russell Kirkpatrick
Elizabeth Knox

Shonagh Koea
John A. Lee
Elsie Locke
Terry Locke
Robert Lord
Edith Lyttleton
Anthony McCarten
Greg McGee
Juliet Marillier
Cilla McQueen
Margaret Mahy
Bill Manhire
Frederick Edward Maning
Phillip Mann
Ged Maybury
Lyn McConchie
Linda McNabb
Katherine Mansfield
Ngaio Marsh
Owen Marshall
Bruce Mason
James McNeish
Richard Meros
Ian Middleton
O. E. Middleton
Geoff Moon
Count Geoffrey Potocki de Montalk
Ronald Hugh Morrieson
Michael J T Morrissey
John Mulgan
Marjory Lydia Nicholls
Michael O'Leary
Ruth Park
Emily Perkins
Bill Pearson (New Zealand writer)
Mark Pirie
Robert J. Pope
Edna Pithie, New Zealand Women writers 1963-70, Founder Tauranga Writers, 1967
Bruce Purchase
Amber Reeves
William Pember Reeves
Lauren Kim Roche
Elspeth Sandys
Frank Sargeson
Duncan Sarkies

Dick Scott
Rosie Scott
Maurice Shadbolt
Keith Sinclair
Nalini Singh
Laura Solomon
C. K. Stead
Jacqui Sturm
Chad Taylor
Philip Temple
Mervyn Thompson
Brian Turner
Hone Tuwhare
Julius Vogel
Joy Watson
Ian Wedde
Peter Wells
Albert Wendt
Cherry Wilder (Cherry Barbara Grimm)
Alison Wong
Niel Wright
Thyra Avis Mary Acres
Pinky Agnew
Pamela Allen
Catherine Ann Andersen
Isabella Smith Andrews
Dorothy Butler
Lynley Dodd
Elizabeth Geertruida Agatha Dyson
Catherine Fulton
Elizabeth Anne Gard'ner
Kirsty Gunn
Sarah Higgins
Eva Esther Hill
Amy Grace Kane
Elizabeth Kelso
Annabel Langbein
Catherine Julia Mackay
Hester Maclean
Katherine Mansfield
Tina Matthews
Elizabeth Messenger
Pérrine Moncrieff
Katherine Elizabeth Morton
Shirley Erena Murray

Margaret Mutu
Lizzie Frost Rattray
Violet Augusta Roche
Adela Blanche Stewart
Ngaire Thomas
Jessica Watson
Joy Watson
Lydia Wevers
Annabelle White
Alistair Campbell (poet)
Kauraka Kauraka
Vela Manusaute
John Pule
Alix Bosco
Freda Bream
Paul Cleave
Neil Cross
Joan Druett
John Dunmore
Dorothy Eden
Dorothy Fowler
Maurice Gee
J
Andrea Jutson
Lindy Kelly
Nigel Latta
Michael Laws
Ngaio Marsh
James McNeish
Paddy Richardson
Mike Riddell
Simon Snow (writer)
Vanda Symon
Chad Taylor (writer)
Paul Thomas (writer)
Joyce West
Catherine Mary Ann Adamson
Charles John Ayton
David Paton Balfour
George Wallace Bollinger
Hannah Rebecca Frances Caverhill
James Cox (labourer)
Catherine Fulton
H. W. Gretton
Sarah Louise Mathew

Catherine Hester Ralfe
George Albert Tuck
Alexander Whisker
Hector Bolitho
Paula Boock
Walter D'Arcy Cresswell
Stevan Eldred-Grigg
David Hartnell
Witi Ihimaera
Annamarie Jagose
Katherine Mansfield
Bill Pearson (New Zealand writer)
rank Sargeson
Hugh Walpole
Peter Wells (filmmaker)
Jeremy Commons
Barry Barclay
Arapera Hineira Kaa Blank
Bub Bridger
Riwia Brown
Harry Dansey
Alan Duff
Wira Gardiner
Patricia Grace
Briar Grace-Smith
Keri Hulme
Ihaia Hutana
Witi Ihimaera
Pei Te Hurinui Jones
Hoani Te Whatahoro Jury
Himiona Tupakihi Kamira
Leslie George Kelly
Reweti Tuhorouta Kohere
Hamuera Tamahau Mahupuku
Rehutai Maihi
Purakau Maika
Max Mariu
Kāterina Mataira
Te Uruhina McGarvey-Tiakiwai
Sidney Moko Mead
Maraea Morete
Paula Morris
Hōri Mahue Ngata
Evelyn Patuawa-Nathan
Hamiora Tumutara Te Tihi-o-te-whenua Pio

Hariata Whakatau Pitini-Morera
Tama Poata
Hemi Potatau
Te Iki-o-te-rangi Pouwhare
Erenora Puketapu-Hetet
Jacqueline Sturm
Robert Sullivan (poet)
Tamairangi
Takaanui Hohaia Tarakawa
Te Hapimana Tauke
Apirana Taylor
Renee Taylor (writer)
Hone Taare Tikao
Hone Tuwhare
Suraya Dewing
Dorothy Fowler
Template:Katherine Mansfield
Template:Juliet Marillier
Archibald Baxter
Edmund Hillary
Philip Temple
Jessica Watson
Herbert Horatio Spencer Westmacott
Michael Bassett
James Cowan
John Dunmore
Matt Elliott (writer)
Eric John Godley
Michael King
Tony Mackle
James McNeish
Paul Moon
Gordon Ogilvie
Harry Ricketts
Keith Sinclair
Sydney Goodsir Smith
Philip Temple
Peter Wells (filmmaker)
Steve Braunias
Phil Gifford
Ian Jorgensen
Richard Long (journalist)
Gary McCormick
Bill Ralston
Brian Rudman

Chris Trotter
Martin van Beynen
Peter Williams (broadcaster)
M. H. Holcroft
Tze Ming Mok
Bill Pearson (New Zealand writer)
Roger Sandall
Flip Grater
Alison Holst
Annabel Langbein
Annabelle White
Willis Thomas Goodwin Airey
Margaret Alington
Johannes Carl Andersen
Austin Graham Bagnall
Tony Ballantyne (historian)
Michael Bassett
John Cawte Beaglehole
Tim Beaglehole
Herries Beattie
James Belich (historian)
Elsdon Best
Judith Binney
John Thomas Blake
James William Brodie
Lindsay Buick
Randal Mathews Burdon
Arthur Gordon Butchers
Alice Candy
Arthur Carman
James Cowan (New Zealand writer)
Gerald Garrick Cunningham
James Wightman Davidson
Janet Davidson
Thomas William Downes
Joan Druett
Alison Edith Hilda Drummond
John Dunmore
Kepa Hamuera Anaha Ehau
Stevan Eldred-Grigg
Peter Entwisle
Roger Curtis Green
Barry Gustafson
Rongowhakaata Pere Halbert
Frederick George Hall-Jones

Joel Hayward
Mary St Domitille Hickey
James Hight
Te Rangi Hīroa
John Houston (New Zealand writer)
Himiona Tupakihi Kamira
Leslie George Kelly
Michael King
Hardwicke Knight
Reweti Tuhorouta Kohere
Stephen Peter Llewellyn
Harold David London
Averil Margaret Lysaght
George Ranald Macdonald
Joseph Angus Mackay
W. David McIntyre
Malcolm McKinnon
W H McLeod
Alexander Hare McLintock
Robert McNab
Sidney Moko Mead
Constant Mews
Caroline Miller (planner)
Paul Moon
William Morley (New Zealand methodist)
William Parker Morrell
Herbert David Mullon
Hoani Nahi
Hensleigh Carthew Marryat Norris
Gordon Ogilvie
W. H. Oliver
Claudia Orange
Vincent Orange (historian)
Glyn Parry (historian)
John Dobrée Pascoe
Morvin Simon
George Conrad Petersen
Jock Phillips
Hamiora Tumutara Te Tihi-o-te-whenua Pio
Hariata Whakatau Pitini-Morera
J. G. A. Pocock
Te Iki-o-te-rangi Pouwhare
Major Albert Rugby Pratt
Christopher Pugsley
William Pember Reeves

Geoffrey Rice
James Basil Wilkie Roberton
Ruth Miriam Ross
Herbert Otto Roth
Anne Salmond
Guy Scholefield
Dick Scott (historian)
William Henry John Seffern
Richard Shannon (historian)
Keith Sinclair
Bernard Sladden
Maxwell James Grant Smart
Stephenson Percy Smith
Duncan Sommerville
Flora Park Cave Spurdle
David Stahel
Hugh Stewart (classical scholar)
Russell Stone
Rory Sweetman
Ronald Syme
Aperahama Taonui
Takaanui Hohaia Tarakawa
Nicholas Tarling
Te Hapimana Tauke
Raniera Te Ahiko
Mohi Te Atahikoia
Wiremu Te Kahui Kararehe
Nopera Te Rangiuia
Tukumana Te Taniwha
Iraia Te Ama-o-te-rangi Te Whaiti
Arthur Saunders Thomson
Mabel Whitaker
Frederick Lloyd Whitfeld Wood
The Work of J.G.A. Pocock
Arthur Henry Adams
Oscar Alpers
Aroha Awarau
Charles Nalder Baeyertz
Louisa Alice Baker
John Ballance
David Ballantyne
Christopher Banks
Harry Barker (mayor)
Constance Barnicoat
Johann Friedrich Wilhelm Baucke

Frederick Baume
Herries Beattie
William Berry (journalist)
James Munro Bertram
William Pierpont Black
John Blumsky
Thomas Bracken
James Benn Bradshaw
Harold Brainsby
John Braithwaite (journalist)
Henry Brett (journalist)
Cameron Brewer
Dick Brittenden
Russell Brown (New Zealand)
David Bruce (minister)
Lindsay Buick
Margaret Bullock
Violet Alberta Jessie Burns
D. J. Cameron
Murray Cammick
Arthur Carman
Christine Cole Catley
Geoff Chapple (writer)
Chiu Kwok-chun
Arthur Clayden
Constance Clyde
Deborah Coddington
Mark Cohen (journalist)
Joseph Colborne-Veel
William Whitehouse Collins
Roger Cook (journalist)
Pam Corkery
Phillip Cottrell
Geoffrey Cox (journalist)
Walter D'Arcy Cresswell
John Crewes
Leonard John Cronin
Ian Cross
Max Cryer
Shayne Currie
William Cutten
John Daly-Peoples
John Daniell (rugby player)
Harry Dansey
Alex de Jong

George E. Dewar
Bernard Diederich
Mary Dreaver
James Mackay Drummond
Oliver Duff
Eileen Duggan
Elizabeth Geertruida Agatha Dyson
Brendon Egan
Mary Teresa Enright
Guyon Espiner
Benjamin Farjeon
David Farrier
George Fenwick
A. N. Field
Derek Fox (broadcaster)
Ebenezer Fox
Charles Fraser (minister)
Alfred Amory George
Phil Gifford
Edward Thomas Gillon
Robert Gilmour (journalist)
Esther Glen
Diana Goodman
Patrick Gower (journalist)
Alfred Augustus Grace
James Gordon Stuart Grant
Grace Winifred Green
H. W. Gretton
Edith Searle Grossmann
Nicky Hager
Robert Coupland Harding
Richard Harman (journalist)
Stella May Henderson
Orton Sutherland Hintz
Alexander Hogg
Robert Hogg (New Zealand politician)
Robert Hogg (socialist)
Tahu Hole
Liddy Holloway
Jim Hopkins
J. T. Marryat Hornsby
Caroline Cadette Howard
John Hudson (journalist)
Graeme Hunt
Robin Hyde

Leonard Isitt (minister)
Ethel May Jacobson
Colin James (journalist)
Bruce Jesson
Amy Grace Kane
Leslie George Kelly
Elizabeth Kelso
Reweti Tuhorouta Kohere
Thomas Lambert (horticulturist)
William Lane
Patrick Anthony Lawlor
Thomson Wilson Leys
John Liddell Kelly
June Margaret Litman
Stephen Peter Llewellyn
Edward Lofley
Richard Long (journalist)
Robert Andrew Loughnan
David Luckie
Wilfrid Mervyn Lusty
Catherine Julia Mackay
Jessie Mackay
Joseph Angus Mackay
Margaret MacPherson
Rehutai Maihi
Jane Mander
John Manning (journalist)
Charles Allan Marris
Samuel McDonald Martin
Elma Maua
John McBeth
David McGill (writer)
Malcolm McKinnon
Terry McLean
Rosemary McLeod
Frederick Walter Gascoyne Miller
Tom Mockridge
Katherine Elizabeth Morton
Alan Edward Mulgan
John Mulgan
William Charles Nation
William Brinsley Nicholson
Joanna Norris
Gregory O'Brien
Brian O'Flaherty

Rod Oram
Michael Otto (journalist)
Tom Paul
Jesse Peach
Nick Perry (journalist)
Noel Pharazyn
Sean Plunket
Charles Quentin Fernie Pope
Charles Purnell
Keith Quinn (broadcaster)
Charles Rae
Bill Ralston
George Eric Oakes Ramsden
Lizzie Frost Rattray
George McCullagh Reed
William Reeves (journalist)
David Robie
Melodie Robinson
Violet Augusta Roche
Hilda Rollett
Forrestina Elizabeth Ross
Derek Round
Brian Rudman
Marcia Russell
Kamahl Santamaria
Guy Scholefield
Dick Scott (historian)
Robyn Scott
Sidney Wilfred Scott
William Henry John Seffern
Phineas Selig
Maurice Shadbolt
John Shrapnell
Dorothy Edith Simons
Barry Soper
Eileen Louise Soper
Charles Southwell
Flora Park Cave Spurdle
Laura Jane Suisted
Dylan Taite
Ian Templeton
Jim Thorn
John Trenwith
William Henry Triggs
Martin van Beynen

Mike Vincent
Neil Waka
Crosbie Ward
Clement Gordon Watson
Jenny Wheeler
William Arthur Whitlock
Harold Williams (linguist)
Peter Williams (broadcaster)
Charles Wilson (librarian)
Robert Burchfield
Hōri Mahue Ngata
Eric Partridge
James Munro Bertram
Charles Brasch
Terry Locke
Michael J T Morrissey
Bill Pearson (New Zealand writer)
Mark Pirie
H. M. Posnett
John Reid (professor of English)
Kendrick Smithyman
C. K. Stead
Lydia Wevers
Niel Wright
Guyon Espiner

Chapter 3

Malenesia

Fijian Writers

Ahmed Ali
Ami Chandra
Brij Lal
Sudesh Mishra
Satendra Nandan
Ayodhya Prasad
Sudesh Mishra
Satendra Nandan
Ayodhya Prasad
Vilsoni Hereniko
Epeli Hau'ofa
Vilsoni Hereniko
Daren Kamali
Prerna Lal
Rusiate Nayacakalou
Dick Watling

33

Chapter 4

New Caledonian Writers

Claudine Jacques
Nicolas Kurtovitch

Chapter 5

Papuan Writers (Indonesia)

No Unknown writers

Chapter 6

Papua New Guinean Writers

Vincent Eri
Beatrice Grimshaw
John Kasaipwalova
Albert Maori Kiki
Ignatius Kilage
John Waiko
Allan Natachee

Chapter 7

Solomon Islands Writers

Rexford Orotaloa
Matila Balekana
Panapasa Balekana

Chapter 8

Vanuatuan writers

Allie Webster
Bill Kautz
Grace Mera Molisa

Chapter 9

Micronesia

Federated States of Micronesian Writers

Luelen Bernart
Emelihter Kihleng

Chapter 10

Guam Writers (United States)

Dirk Ballendorf
Tony Palomo

Chapter 11

Kiribati Writers

Abureti Takaio
Keina Tito
Teresia Teaiwa

Chapter 12

Marshall Islands Writers

Unknown Writers

Chapter 13

Nauruan Writers

Margaret Hendrie
Joanne Gobure

Chapter 14

Northern Mariana Islands Writers (United States)

Unknown Writers

Chapter 15

Palauan Writers

Valentine Namio Sengebau

Chapter 16

Wake Island Writers (United States)

Unknown Writers

Chapter 17

Polynesia

American Samoan Writers (United States)

Sia Figiel
George Pratt (missionary)
Teo Tuvale
Albert Wendt
Savea Sano Malifa
Aiono Fanaafi Le Tagaloa
George Pratt (missionary)
Teo Tuvale
Albert Wendt
Tusiata Avia
Sapa'u Ruperake Petaia
Albert Wendt
Emma Kruse Va'ai
Aiono Fanaafi Le Tagaloa

Chapter 18

Cook Islands (New Zealand)

Kauraka Kauraka
Florence Frisbie
Alistair Te Ariki Campbell
Tom Davis
Lydia Davis

Chapter 19

Easter Island Writers

Unknown Writers

Chapter 20

French Polynesian (France)

Henri Hiro
Célestine Hitiura Vaite
Marco Namouro

Chapter 21

Hawaiian Writers (United States)

Isabella Abbott
Jeff Chang (journalist)
Sam Choy
Kiana Davenport
Samuel Kamakau
Mahealani Perez-Wendt
Kiana Tom
Haunani-Kay Trask
Mililani Trask
Kirby Wright
Danny Yamashiro
Lilikalā Kameʻeleihiwa
George Kanahele
Herb Kawainui Kāne
Elizabeth Kekaaniau
Liliuokalani
Nancy Kahalewai
Kalākaua
Jacob O. Adler
Kirk Allen
Kristina Anapau
David Dwight Baldwin
Allan Beekman
Rynn Berry
Don Blanding
Linda Boyden
O. A. Bushnell
Joseph Campbell
William Richards Castle, Jr.
Makana Risser Chai
Jeff Chang (journalist)
Patrick Ching
Eric Chock
Pam Chun
Kiana Davenport
Frank Marshall Davis
Gavan Daws
Charles Fletcher Dole
Edmund Pearson Dole
Gregg Doyel

Leon Edel

51

Nathaniel Bright Emerson
Eric Paul Shaffer
William Finnegan
R. Barri Flowers
Walter F. Frear
David Gallaher
Allegra Goodman
Lauren Graham
Glen Grant (historian)
William Lowthian Green
Ron Jacobs (broadcaster)
Nancy Kahalewai
Dennis Kamakahi
Lilikalā Kameʻeleihiwa
Herb Kawainui Kāne
Kaui Hart Hemmings
Elizabeth Kekaaniau
Nora Okja Keller
Nanci Kincaid
Robert Kiyosaki
Fletcher Knebel
Juliet Kono
Ah Jook Ku
George Parsons Lathrop
Liliuokalani
John C. Lilly
Lois Lowry
Ian MacMillan (author)
Mahealani Dudoit
April Masini
Lisa Matsumoto
Chris McKinney
W. S. Merwin
Jason Momoa
Rodney Morales
Laura Moriarty (novelist)
Katy Munger
Milton Murayama
Kathleen Norris (poet)
Gary Pak
Mark Panek
Albert Saijo
Tara Bray Smith
Maya Soetoro-Ng

David Stannard

Frank Stewart (poet)
Kiana Tom
Lee Tonouchi
Haunani-Kay Trask
Armine von Tempski
Henry Martyn Whitney
Robert Wintner
Norman Wong
Kirby Wright
Lois-Ann Yamanaka
Danny Yamashiro
Helen Desha Beamer
Mahi Beamer
Winona Beamer
Mark Keali‘i Ho‘omalu
Kalākaua
Kui Lee
Leleiohoku II
Likelike
Liliuokalani
Lunalilo
Keola Beamer
Khalil Fong
Amy Hānaiali‘i Gilliom
Don Ho
Jack Johnson (musician)
Israel Kamakawiwo‘ole
Eric Lee (musician)
Glenn Medeiros
John Oszajca
Dean Pitchford
Keali‘i Reichel
Louis Keouli Thompson
Jason Tom

Chapter 22

Niuean Writers (New Zealand)

Nelisi, Lino
Vela Manusaute
John Pule

Chapter 23

Pitcairn Islands Writers (United Kingdom)

Nadine Christian

Chapter 24

Samoan Writers

Aiono Fanaafi Le Tagaloa
George Pratt
Albert Wendt
Autagavaia Tipi Autagavaia
Autagavaia Tipi Autagavaia
Savea Sano Malifa
Sapa'u Ruperake Petaia
Caroline Sinavaiana-Gabbard
Robert Louis Stevenson
Teo Tuvale
Savea Sano Malifa
Sia Figiel

Chapter 25

Tongan Writers

Sione Lātūkefu
Epeli Hau'ofa

57
Chapter 26

Tuvaluan Writers

Susie Saitala Kofe
Suamalie N.T. Iosefa

Chapter 27

Wallis and Futuna Islands Writers (France)

Marco Namouro (1889-1968), writer.
Célestine Hitiura Vaite (born 1966), writer.

www.ingramcontent.com/pod-product-compliance
Ingram Content Group UK Ltd.
Pitfield, Milton Keynes, MK11 3LW, UK
UKHW041915190726
13854UKWH00003B/1256